The Waterman/Harewood Piano Series

Recital Repertoire Book One

selected and edited by

Fanny Waterman
and
Marion Harewood

GW00643093

Faber Music Limited

London

CONTENTS

This collection © 1981 by Faber Music Ltd
First published in 1981 by Faber Music Ltd
3 Queen Square London WC1N 3AU
Printed in England by Halstan & Co Ltd
Reprinted 1984

INTRODUCTION

The twenty-eight pieces in this collection span a period of about two hundred years, and have been chosen to present a range of different styles and forms from most of the major composers of the piano repertoire. We have specified, where appropriate, the collection, sonata or suite from which a piece is taken.

We strongly recommend that pianists should, when studying any piece, make a point of learning more about the composer's life and background, the period he lived in and what other music he wrote. The pieces in this collection should also lead to the study of, for example, the form and function of a *bourrée* in a baroque suite or partita, the shape of a classical rondo, or the character of *alla breve* time. Knowledge of the different types of keyboard instruments used by each composer and their different mechanisms and sounds is of great value in interpreting the music.

Wherever possible we have worked from Urtext editions, but we have also used our musical judgement and experience to give interpretative guidance. In the case of the works by J.S. Bach, decisions over speed, dynamics and phrasing have been left to each pianist, as was usual in Bach's time. Nor have we added phrase marks to the Scarlatti sonata, but instead have inserted commas to show the length of each phrase; these help to punctuate the music and should be treated as if taking a new breath without disturbing the flow and shape of the melody. For Schumann's pieces we have also kept to the original text, but have added some pedal marks for guidance.

The importance of careful fingering cannot be over-emphasized: it is the basis for a secure technique and an important factor in producing the correct quality of sound. As Chopin wrote: 'each finger is built differently; each has a different strength and function. One must not destroy, but rather should develop, the finesse of touch that is proper and natural to each finger.' The fingerings in this volume attempt to follow these principles. At first sight some may seem unorthodox, but closer study should reveal the reason in each case. The main consideration must always be the placing of stronger or weaker fingers in the musically and technically appropriate places. Correct fingering will assist the development of: a feeling of security; reliable memorizing; clear articulation in fast passages; the easing of awkward passages; correct phrasing; avoiding misplaced stresses; rhythmic vitality; good chord balance; clear part-playing; variety of textures; a good sonority. The differences in size, shape and power of each pair of hands will determine the final choice of fingering.

The use of the pedal is more difficult to define, and indeed most composers have written pedal indications only where they wish to make a particular point about sonority. This does not mean that the pedal should not be used at other times, but that it should be left to the discretion of each performer. Pianos and acoustics vary so widely that players must be prepared not only to adjust their pedalling to different circumstances but also to make small alterations in tempo to achieve clarity of sound. We therefore felt it inadvisable to insert too many pedal indications. In practising it is important to work out a careful pedalling plan, but is equally important to practise without the pedal to ensure finger legato, accuracy in skips and good chord balance. The pedal should only be used to enhance the sound, not as a means of covering untidy playing.

F.W.
M.H.

2 Bourrées

from *French Overture*, BWV 831
aus *Ouvertüre nach französischer Art*

JOHANN SEBASTIAN BACH
(1685–1750)

1.

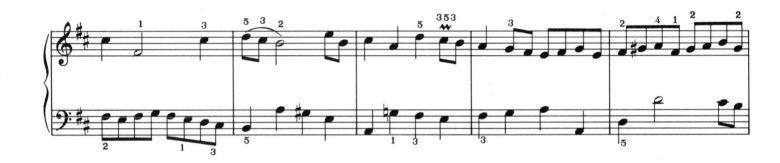

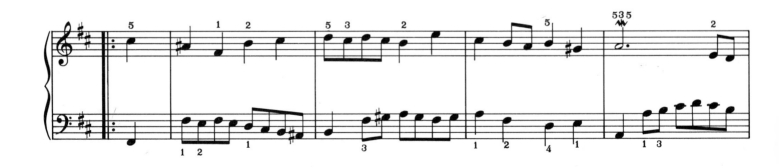

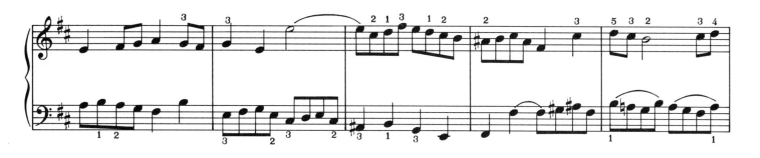

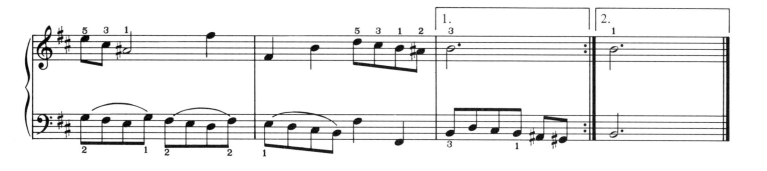

2.

Bourrée I da capo

Echo

from *French Overture,* BWV 831
aus *Ouvertüre nach französischer Art*

JOHANN SEBASTIAN BACH
(1685–1750)

Solfeggietto

CARL PHILIPP EMANUEL BACH
(1714–1788)

Allegro con brio

above r.h.

Sonata

L.433, K.446

DOMENICO SCARLATTI
(1685–1757)

Pastorale, allegrissimo *

*'Allegrissimo', the composer's own marking, can best be translated as 'light-hearted' and is therefore as indication of mood rather than speed.

Finale

Sonata in D, Hob. XVI: 37

JOSEPH HAYDN
(1732–1809)

Presto ma non troppo

Da capo sin al segno ℅

sempre staccato

Piano Piece

Klavierstück

(1766)

WOLFGANG AMADEUS MOZART
(1756–1791)

Allegretto

Allegro
(1763)

WOLFGANG AMADEUS MOZART
(1756–1791)

Fantasia

KV 397

WOLFGANG AMADEUS MOZART
(1756–1791)

Allegretto

Bagatelle

Op. 33, no. 3

LUDWIG VAN BEETHOVEN
(1770–1827)

Allegretto

Nocturne No. 5

H 37

JOHN FIELD
(1782–1837)

Cantabile

FREDERIC CHOPIN
(1810–1849)

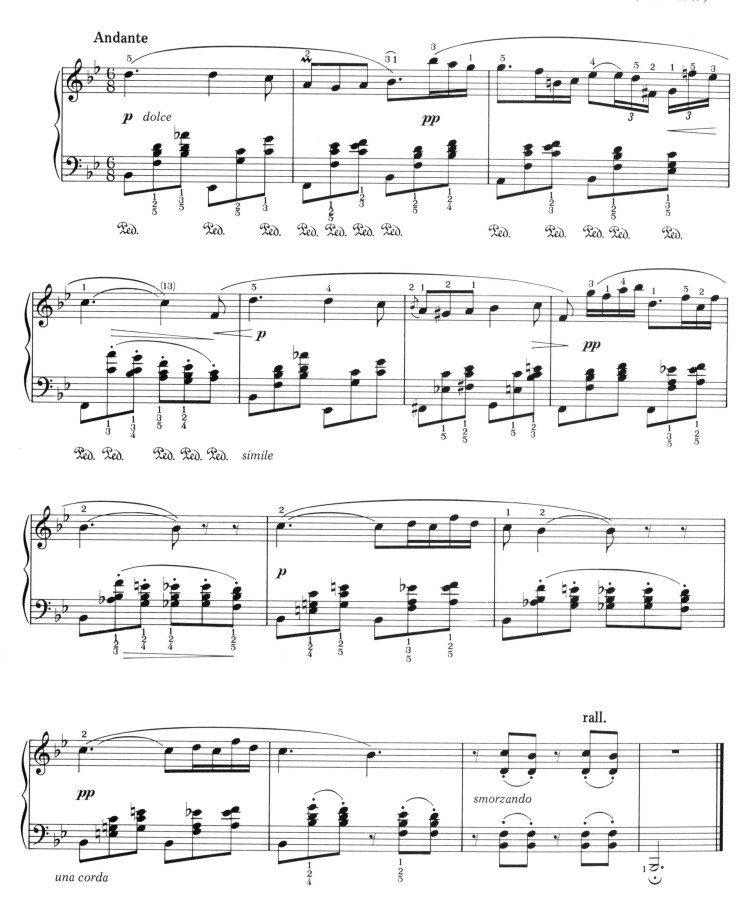

Prelude
Op. 28 no. 4

FREDERIC CHOPIN
(1810–1849)

Prelude

Op. 28 no. 6

FREDERIC CHOPIN
(1810–1849)

Lento assai

Prelude

Op. 28 no. 20

FREDERIC CHOPIN
(1810–1849)

Venetian Gondola Song

Venezianisches Gondellied

from *Songs without Words*, Op. 19
aus *Lieder ohne Worte*

FELIX MENDELSSOHN
(1809–1847)

Fantasy Dance

from *Album Leaves*, Op. 124
aus *Albumblätter*

Phantasietanz

ROBERT SCHUMANN
(1810–1856)

Sehr rasch *(molto allegro)*

May, dear May

from *Album for the Young,* Op. 68
aus *Album für die Jugend*

Mai, lieber Mai

ROBERT SCHUMANN
(1810–1856)

Nicht schnell *(Non troppo Allegro)*

Knight Rupert

Knecht Ruprecht

from *Album for the Young* Op. 68
aus *Album für die Jugend*

ROBERT SCHUMANN
(1810–1856)

50

from *Album for the Young*, Op. 68
aus *Album für die Jugend*

ROBERT SCHUMANN
(1810–1856)

Waltz

Op. 39 no. 11

JOHANNES BRAHMS
(1833–1897)

Song of the Lark

Das Lerchenlied

from *Children's Album,* Op. 39
aus *Album für die Kinder*

PETER IL'YCH TCHAIKOWSKY
(1840–1893)

April: Snowdrops

April: Schneeglöckchen

from *The Seasons,* Op. 37
aus *den Jahreszeiten*

PETER IL'YCH TCHAIKOWSKY
(1840–1893)

Allegretto con moto e un poco rubato

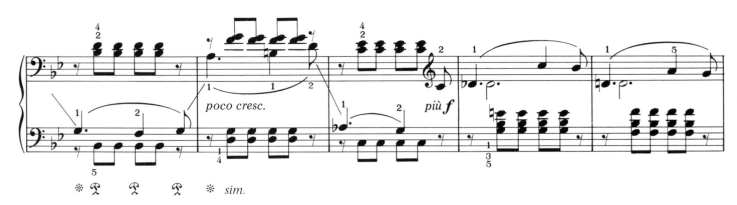

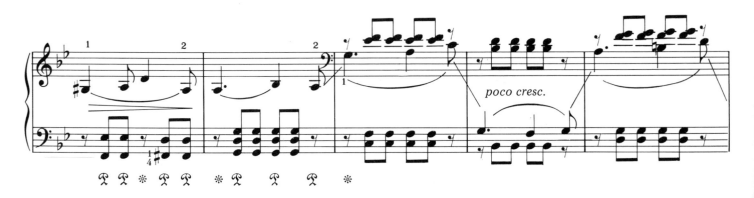

The Little Negro

Le petit Nègre – Der kleine Neger

CLAUDE DEBUSSY
(1862–1918)

An old Musical Box

Où l'on entend une vieille boîte à musique – Wie die Spieldose tönt

DÉODAT DE SÉVERAC
(1872–1921)

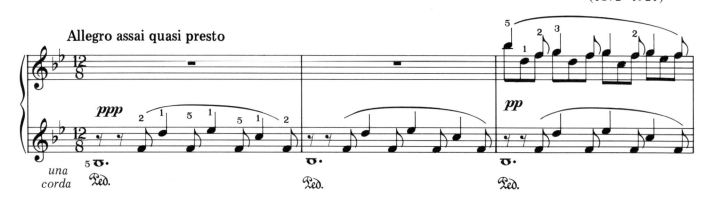

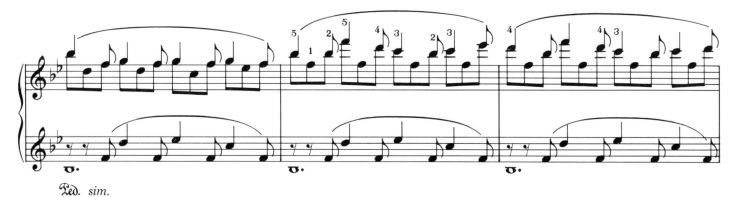

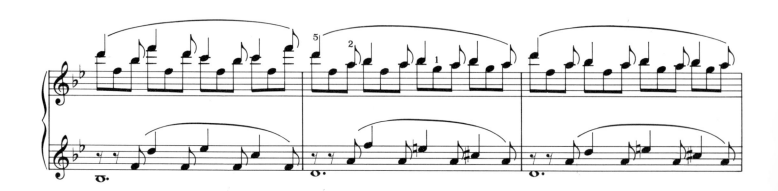

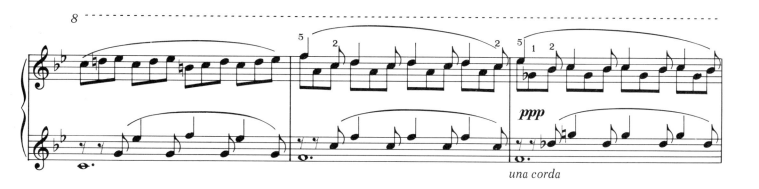

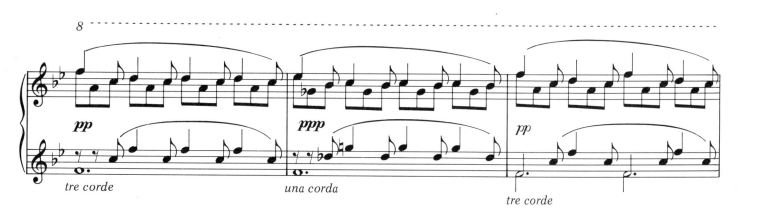